WEIRD

DISAPPEARANCES

TRUE STORIES

Real Tales of Missing People

TOM MCCARTHY

Nomad Press
A division of Nomad Communications
10 9 8 7 6 5 4 3 2 1
Copyright © 2017 by Nomad Press. All rights reserved.
No part of this book may be reproduced in any form without permission in
writing from the publisher, except by a reviewer who may quote brief passages
in a review or **for limited educational use**. The trademark "Nomad Press"
and the Nomad Press logo are trademarks of Nomad Communications, Inc.

This book was manufactured by CGB Printers,
North Mankato, Minnesota, United States
May 2017, Job #221361
ISBN Softcover: 978-1-61930-530-4
ISBN Hardcover: 978-1-61930-526-7

Educational Consultant, Marla Conn

Questions regarding the ordering of this book should be addressed to
Nomad Press
2456 Christian St.
White River Junction, VT 05001
www.nomadpress.net

Printed in the United States.

MIX
Paper from
responsible sources
FSC® C008080

Contents

More titles in the
Mystery & Mayhem Series

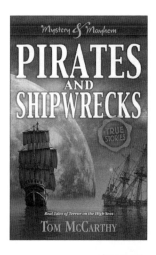

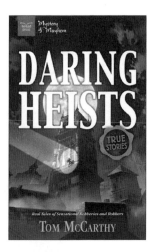

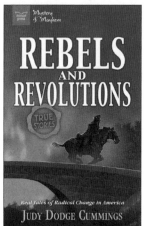

Introduction
Where Did They Go?

It's a simple enough question.
Where did they go?

Here is a thought that might seem strange since you are holding a book filled with stories about mysterious disappearances. There is no such thing as "disappearing." People have to go somewhere. They don't vaporize into thin air. It is just that no one knows exactly where they went.

That is what makes this book so interesting.

Take the story of Virginia Dare. When Virginia Dare was born on the steamy island of Roanoke in 1587, she was the first baby in what settlers called the New World. The colonists who welcomed her saw the smiling baby as a sign of hope that they would make it. That hope would not last. Where did the entire colony disappear to? More than 400 years later, historians are still trying to answer that question.

Or what about Anastasia Romanov? In 1918, revolutionaries overthrew the Russian monarchy and murdered Tsar Nicholas II and his family— Anastasia among them. But afterward, no one could find Anastasia's body. Did she somehow survive her execution?

Have you heard of Amelia Earhart? She was a daredevil hero who flew her airplane everywhere. The entire world loved her sense of adventure and her smiles and bravery in the face of danger. When she announced her plan to fly around the world in 1937, the whole world buzzed with excitement. She confidently guided her plane off the runway toward the horizon and—was never heard from again.

Solomon Northup was an African American at a time when many African Americans were slaves. They were treated no better than farm animals by their white owners. Solomon Northup lived in the North as a free man. That changed quickly when he was tricked, kidnapped, and sold as a slave. He then spent 12 years as a piece of property. Even after he escaped back to freedom, fate intervened again when he disappeared after giving a lecture to the public. Was he captured again? Killed? Did he simply decide to live a quiet life?

Percy Fawcett was an explorer. He had subjected himself to years of torturous slogging through the dangerous jungles of South America and came close to death many times. Along the way, he claimed to have seen many very unusual things, such as dogs with two noses. Stories about a lost city of unimaginable wealth drew him back to the jungle. But he should not have tested his luck. He returned one final time to find the lost city. That was a mistake. No one ever saw him again.

Ready to take a journey into the mysterious world of the unknown? Maybe you'll unearth some answers to these historical mysteries!

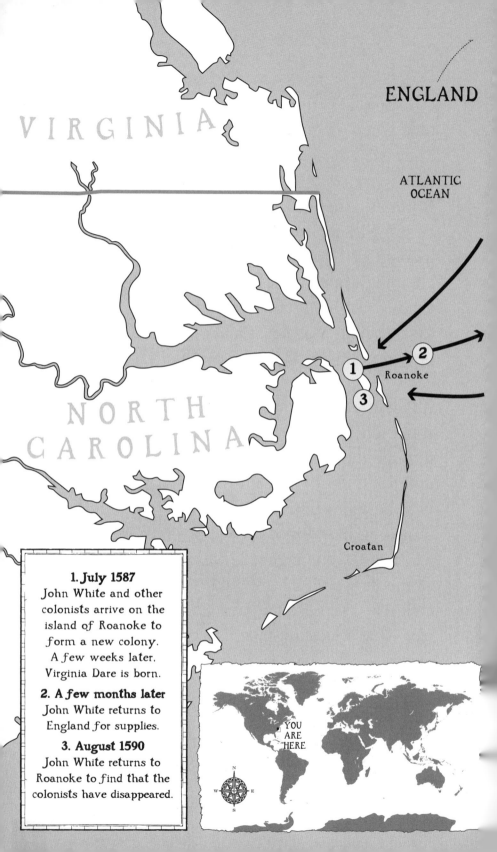

ENGLAND

ATLANTIC
OCEAN

VIRGINIA

NORTH
CAROLINA

Roanoke

Croatan

1. July 1587
John White and other
colonists arrive on the
island of Roanoke to
form a new colony.
A few weeks later,
Virginia Dare is born.

2. A few months later
John White returns to
England for supplies.

3. August 1590
John White returns to
Roanoke to find that the
colonists have disappeared.

YOU
ARE
HERE

Chapter One
Virginia Dare

For the English settlers in the colony of
Roanoke, the birth of Virginia Dare was the
beginning of a new era of health and wealth.
Or so they hoped.

But history isn't always nice to new settlers.

Virginia Dare was born in 1587, just two
weeks after her parents, Eleanor and Ananias
Dare, landed on an island in the New World.
Roanoke Island lay between the coast of what
is now North Carolina and a small group of
outer islands. The Dare family and more than
120 other men, women, and children had sailed
from England in search of a better life.

Everyone was excited that a new baby had been born in the New World, but at the same time, they felt nervous. The place they now called home was not very welcoming. The forest was so thick that sunlight barely reached the moist, mossy ground. Supplies were scarce. People were scared.

There is danger lurking out there, they thought.

The colonists had survived a rough ocean voyage and two weeks of hard living on new land. Except, it wasn't exactly new land. Another group of settlers had lived there two years before. Those settlers had left behind cabins and a crumbling fort. They hadn't succeeded in establishing a colony. Where did they go? Why had their settlement failed?

Here's what happened. The English people in the earlier settlement did not appreciate that others already lived there. These "other people" had been living on that land comfortably, peacefully, and productively for many years.

The Native Americans who lived there knew and loved the land and what it offered. At first, they welcomed these strange new English people, hoping they could all share in the abundance that surrounded them.

The two groups traded goods. The English needed deer and bison skins, which the Native Americans gave them in exchange for knives, hatchets, and colorful glass beads. It seemed to be a good deal for both, each getting something they wanted but did not have.

Soon enough, however, things began to get tense. Mistrust settled in. The English were unused to surviving off the land. They were running out of food. They were hungry.

While trying to get more food, the English killed one of the Native Americans who had been helping them. And that was the end of the peaceful arrangement. The English had to get off the island quickly, before their hosts sought revenge. They left behind their houses and a small fort built from the strong pine trees of the lush forest.

Now, two years later, a new group of settlers would try to succeed where the first had failed.

A man named John White was the driving force behind this new settlement. He was a friend of the famous Sir Walter Raleigh, an English knight with big plans to expand English territories. Sir Walter was a favorite of Queen Elizabeth, who wanted more than anything to increase the size of her empire. The queen had the power and, more importantly, she had a lot of money.

What she needed was people. She needed people who were brave enough and adventurous enough to want to pick up everything and move to a new land thousands of miles from home. Would you have volunteered?

John White had visited Roanoke with the first group, but he had been lucky enough to leave before the troubles began. He had liked what he saw and was willing to try again.

John White was a great talker. He could persuade a pig to take a bath! John White talked to anyone in England who would listen about the hope and dreams and comfort that were waiting for them in the New World. He probably didn't mention much about what happened with the Native Americans. He painted a picture of the wealth and riches that were far beyond anything people had in London, where it was crowded and dirty.

Whatever he said made Roanoke and the New World sound as if they were worth the risk of a long ocean voyage and uncertain early days.

John White was so convincing that he even talked his daughter, Eleanor, and her husband, Ananias, into making the dangerous trip. John White's stories of the beautiful land that lay ahead were so magical that Eleanor and Ananias left their two young children behind in England. Once they settled in the New World, they could send for the youngsters and they would all live happily together.

They would never be reunited, though. People are still trying to figure out why, more than 400 years later.

First, the trip across the Atlantic Ocean was difficult. More than 100 people were crammed onto a small ship that pitched and rolled and seemed to take forever to get anywhere. Their quarters were cramped and there never seemed to be enough fresh air down below.

When John White's new group finally arrived on shore and felt the steadiness of solid land after months of rolling and sliding on the boat, they felt more hopeful. But Roanoke Island was not London. The air was damp and sticky and hotter than anything they had ever felt before. Even breathing was different than it had been in London. Would it stay like this all year? The quiet place was filled with irritating bugs that bit and caused everyone's skin to swell and turn red. There were snakes—the settlers had to be careful about lifting up loose logs.

Their hardscrabble lives in London had not been happy, but at least they knew what to expect. Here, on this island, they had no idea what might happen.

It's a good thing these people were not complainers. They were adventurers! They would make the most of this new land, and they would thrive and be happier than they ever had been at home. At least, that's what they told themselves.

The day after they landed, the settlers marched to the north of Roanoke and found what was left of the first settlement. They watched as deer strolled within the shabby walls of the fort. They saw that vegetables planted by the first group were still thriving, though overgrown. Deer were feeding on them. It was an incredible sight.

They also found the remains of the small cottages that had once provided shelter to earlier settlers. These shaky remnants were all that remained of the first settlers.

John White, always the smooth talker, told the new group of settlers they were lucky to have these ready-made shelters they could fix up. It was much better than starting from scratch, he told them. Otherwise, they would have to cut down trees and build each new house piece by piece in this hot, buggy air. He put a positive spin on things. It was not much, but it was something. People cheered up a little.

Soon, the sounds of hammering and sawing and the bustle of excited people happy to be starting something promising filled the settlement.

John White took time from his work and wrote to a friend back in England that the new group of excited and ambitious colonists "were ready for the untapped riches that North Carolina offered." He was "determined to success for the glory of the Queen and Sir Walter Raleigh."

But then, while digging around the fort, two of the new settlers found human bones scattered in a mossy corner away from where most of the others were working. Whose bones were these? How did this person die? Why weren't they given a proper burial? The discovery startled the settlers. How dangerous was this place?

The shabbiness of the rundown cottages and the fort that was barely standing was one thing. Bones of a dead person was another. It was almost as if the skeleton spoke to them from his crumbling grave: Beware!

Would they be next in this line of failures?

Still, the new settlers had lots of work to do to keep their minds off death and danger. The settlers managed to keep feeling hopeful until a man named George Howe went into the forest.

George Howe had lived in an uncomfortable, foul-smelling apartment in an area of London that itself was horribly crowded and cramped. John White's descriptions of the New World had appealed to George Howe immediately, and he had signed up for the trip without hesitation.

George Howe had been told by John White not to go into the forest alone. Everyone was to walk in groups for protection. But George Howe was excited about seeing the vast expanse of forest and the clear streams that ran through it. He decided not to wait for the others. He went off to enjoy the beauty and freshness of this new land he now called home, so far from the open sewers and rat-infested alleyways near his old London apartment.

George Howe felt he was in paradise and he could not wait to see it any longer.

George Howe left the busy encampment and the steady beat of hammering and sawing and slipped into the quiet forest. After half a mile along a path leading to the calm blue bay, he came to a babbling stream near the shoreline. He decided to catch some crabs, which he had tasted for the first time only two days ago. They had been delicious and fresh.

He took off his clothes and waded into the cool running water, looking beyond the worn rocks for his tasty dinner. The peace and quiet of the moment were things he had dreamed about in London and during the long, hard trip.

Hidden in the reeds along the creek crouched a handful of Native American Secotan warriors. They had come across the calm expanse of the bay from the mainland to see what all the activity was. They were worried that the English had come back, and they were right.

More English, they thought. More trouble. The last time a group of English settlers had been there, one of the members of their tribe had been killed.

The Native Americans saw George Howe and decided now was the time for revenge.

Making sure George Howe was alone, they crept quietly to the edge of the streambank. Then, they pulled sharpened arrows from their quivers and placed them in their bows. Drawing back until the drawstrings seemed about to break, they sent the arrows on their way.

George Howe was struck by sixteen arrows before he knew what had hit him. He fell screaming into the calm water of the creek. Before he could sink to the bottom, the Secotan warriors were on him, hammering his head with rocks and war clubs.

Downstream, the water quickly turned red.

George Howe was dead. His body sank to the rocky bottom of the stream, his arm waving in the current, as if he were saying goodbye.

The bloody and violent death of George Howe was a profound shock to John White and the colonists. Things would never be the same.

The New World no longer seemed a place of beauty. People were cautious. Perhaps Roanoke was a bad idea.

Then, Virginia Dare was born, and she gave the settlers a renewed sense of hope. Virginia Dare, the bright and happy baby, was a welcome addition to the community. She was the first sign that this ambitious plan to settle in a new and unknown land would work.

Virginia Dare was like a new root of a plant that would grow and become strong.

The settlers celebrated the birth of the baby and the fact that they had made great progress on the buildings. The celebrations cheered everyone after the difficult weeks following George Howe's death.

Still, they were unprepared for life in the New World. Apparently, the experiences of the first settlers had taught them nothing. Food began running short. They couldn't turn to the Native Americans for help—the first group of English settlers had made sure that wasn't an option.

John White and the other leaders of the colony met and discussed what to do. There seemed to be only one solution: Someone had to return to England, raise more money, buy more supplies and food, and return to Roanoke as quickly as possible.

If they were lucky, the whole trip could be done in three months. Help would arrive just as spring was settling back in on Roanoke Island.

The settlers who stayed behind and waited for help and new supplies would have the protection of the rebuilt fort and the comfort of the refinished cottages. It seemed like a solid plan.

John White, who had a strong friendship with Sir Walter Raleigh, would certainly be able to raise the money quickly. The leaders of the settlement thought he should be one of the people to go to England. He would return to Roanoke in time to keep the colony alive and growing.

John White was torn, of course. He did not want to leave the colony. Certainly, he did not want to leave his daughter and baby granddaughter.

However, he had started this whole thing and he was responsible for the safety of the settlers. He reluctantly agreed to return to England for help.

John White truly believed he would be back by spring.

Before he boarded his ship, he told those he was leaving behind to be careful. He warned them not to anger the Native Americans. Be respectful.

John White pointed out a tall, wide tree near the shoreline. If you have to leave quickly, if anything goes wrong, carve a cross in this tree, he said. If I see the cross when I return, I will know you left in a hurry, and I will find you on the mainland or another island. If I see the cross, I will know there has been a problem.

He told the settlers that if they found themselves in trouble, the best thing to do was to get across the bay to an island to the south of Roanoke called Croatoan. The Native Americans who lived on Croatoan had been friendly to the English in the past. John While hoped they would be again.

John White left Roanoke with a heavy heart. As he boarded the ship that would take him back to England, he turned to the small gathering of settlers who had come down to the shore to see him off. Be safe, he reminded them. I will be back with everything we need to thrive on Roanoke. Remember Croatoan.

As his ship sailed out from the shore, John White watched as his daughter, Eleanor, holding young Virginia Dare, waved sadly from the shoreline.

Good leaders need to be able to think of things that can go wrong and make plans to avoid them. John White was a good leader. His plan to return to Roanoke with more food and more help was a good one. His idea to carve the warning cross into the tree was a smart one. His plan to have the settlers get to safety on Croatoan in an emergency was a fine one.

The problem with plans is that they can go wrong.

John White made it to England after a hard winter voyage. But complications set in immediately. England was at war with Spain. There were no ships available to return to Roanoke. There was no extra money to buy the food and seeds and supplies for the lonely settlers waiting for him.

Anyone who might have been able to help was focused on the war. It was as if Roanoke no longer mattered.

John White, terrified about what might be happening back on Roanoke, was stuck in England. He stayed there—powerless and full of worry—for three long years.

John White never gave up. There was never a single day that John White did not think of his family and other settlers on Roanoke and what they might be doing. Unfortunately, he could do nothing but hope they were safe. He could only pray there were no problems. He could only wish that if there were problems, Eleanor and Ananias and Virginia Dare and all the others who had put so much trust in him would make their way to Croatoan.

Finally, John White was able to find a ship and set sail to Roanoke. The voyage back seemed to take forever. He could not wait to see his hardy group of settlers and his beautiful granddaughter again. Would she be walking when he saw her? Talking? Would she know him?

When he stepped back on the island after such a long absence, everything was quiet. Too quiet, he thought. No one came to the shore to greet him. There was not a single soul on the island.

The first thing John White looked for was the tree he had shown the settlers as he left. There was no cross on it. That meant the settlers had never felt a sense of danger.

But where were they?

As he walked to the settlement, John White noticed that all the houses had been dismantled in an orderly fashion. The settlers, it seemed, had calmly taken the houses down and packed them away for moving. But to where?

He looked to what had been the edge of the small village and saw the word "CROATOAN" carved on a fence post.

That crude sign was all that remained of 80 men, 17 women, and 11 children—including his granddaughter. Virginia Dare had been the hope and pride of Roanoke. But Roanoke would come to be known as the "Lost Colony."

Had they gone to Croatoan? Were they safe and thriving? Had they been lost at sea trying?

John White was trapped on Roanoke Island by bad weather and leaky ships. He could not get to Croatoan, which was 50 miles away to the south. While that's a short distance by today's standards, for John White, it was impossible. He was tortured by the thought of his family living so close, yet unreachable.

John White never learned what happened to the colonists of Roanoke. When he finally returned to England, he still didn't know the answer. He never fully recovered from his loss and never again sailed to the New World. For the rest of his life, he deeply mourned the loss of Roanoke Colony.

He especially felt the loss of Virginia Dare.

Some reports say that the settlers made it to Croatoan and learned to live and love the land as the Native Americans did. Other reports say that they were lost at sea or had been killed in a battle with the Native Americans. Another report said that that Virginia Dare married "an Indian King" and lived a full and happy life.

Whatever happened, the mystery of Virginia Dare and her adventurous parents and their fellow settlers sparked generations of future immigrants to explore the New World.

WHAT ELSE HAPPENED IN 1587?

- King Philip II of Spain has been plotting to overthrow Queen Elizabeth of England. He plans to put Mary, queen of Scotland, on the throne as a replacement. Queen Elizabeth has Queen Mary beheaded to prevent this switch from happening, which increases tensions between Spain and England so much that a war breaks out.

- Shakespeare is believed to have left his hometown of Stratford-upon-Avon, England, and headed for the big city of London to embark on his career as a playwright and actor.

- On October 18, Spanish Captain Pedro de Unamuno discovers the area that later becomes California.

- Construction begins on the Rialto Bridge in Venice, Italy, which is one of four bridges that span the Grand Canal. Two rows of shops line this pedestrian bridge.

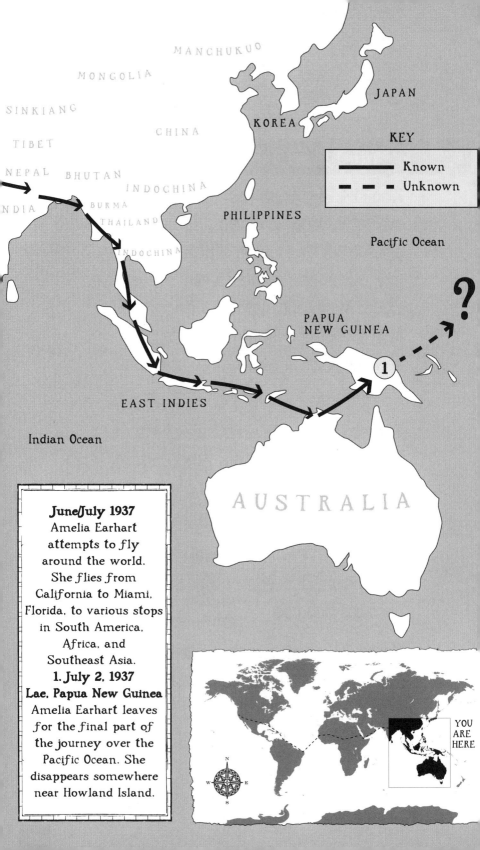

MANCHUKUO

MONGOLIA

SINKIANG

JAPAN

TIBET

CHINA

KOREA

NEPAL   BHUTAN

INDOCHINA

KEY

INDIA

BURMA

—————— Known

THAILAND

- - - - Unknown

INDOCHINA

PHILIPPINES

Pacific Ocean

PAPUA
NEW GUINEA

?

EAST INDIES

①

Indian Ocean

AUSTRALIA

June/July 1937
Amelia Earhart
attempts to fly
around the world.
She flies from
California to Miami,
Florida, to various stops
in South America,
Africa, and
Southeast Asia.
1. July 2, 1937
Lae, Papua New Guinea
Amelia Earhart leaves
for the final part of
the journey over the
Pacific Ocean. She
disappears somewhere
near Howland Island.

YOU
ARE
HERE

N
W   E
S

Chapter Two

The Natural

Amelia Earhart was 23 years old when she took her first airplane ride. Lifting off the ground and soaring into the endless sky over Long Beach, California, the rickety plane shook and the clouds felt like they were rushing in. High above the earth, Amelia Earhart found the thing she loved more than anything—flying. There was nothing like it.

When the plane rolled to a stop on the bumpy airfield, she realized she had not stopped smiling the entire time she was in the air. Amelia Earhart knew what she wanted to do with the rest of her life.

She knew she was born to fly.

Amelia Earhart was born in Atchison, Kansas, on July 24, 1897. As a kid, Amelia Earhart was determined and curious. She always seemed to have an itch that she could not quite scratch—and that led her always to want to try something new. She was restless!

Early in her life, Amelia Earhart knew that if she wanted something done, she had to do it herself. She loved her father and knew he tried hard, but he'd get a new job, get fired, and it would be time to move again. All that moving gave Amelia Earhart a sense of independence.

In 1897, the world moved slowly. There were no cars. People got around in carriages pulled by horses. A three-mile trip down the road was a major expedition that required planning and preparation.

And there were no airplanes. The thought of a flying machine seemed like pure fantasy in 1897. That is just a crazy idea, most people thought.

Not that Amelia Earhart needed cars and airplanes to find adventure. She found it everywhere. She and her sister, Muriel, did anything to keep the boredom away. Amelia Earhart climbed the highest trees in town. She hunted rats with a rifle her father had given her. In winter, she always wanted to be the fastest kid on a sled rushing downhill on snowy mornings.

Amelia Earhart took great chances that made other children gasp. Once, on a trip to St. Louis, Missouri, she had seen a towering, thrilling roller coaster. Back at home, she built a ramp and tied it to the roof of a shed in the back yard. She blasted down the ramp on a sled made from parts of a box and shot into the air, landing with a crash. She cut her lip, tore her dress, and was shaken to the point of dizziness.

Instead of being scared, the rough landing exhilarated her. It thrilled her! She wanted more of it. She climbed right back up to the roof of the shed to try it again.

That ramp was Amelia Earhart's first taste of flying. She didn't know it then, but flying would be both the thing she loved most in the world and the thing that took her out of the world.

Amelia Earhart was fascinated by travel. Some of the places she visited included Toronto, Chicago, Boston, and parts of Kansas, where she was born. Traveling made her eyes bulge out from excitement.

As a young girl, Amelia Earhart began a scrapbook. She pasted newspaper clippings in it about interesting people and events. Almost all these stories were about women who were successful in areas that men usually dominated—which was just about everything. She followed stories about women who were movie producers, lawyers, company presidents, and engineers.

Her first Christmas vacation after graduating from high school in 1916 was spent visiting her sister in Toronto, Canada. Wounded soldiers were coming home from World War I, so she volunteered to help the nurses caring for the patients.

Many of the injured soldiers were pilots— Amelia Earhart quickly became friends with them. She loved their stories about shooting through the clouds and looking down at villages and hills from above.

She often went to a nearby airport to watch pilots taking off and landing. The magic of flying was captivating.

One afternoon, Amelia Earhart and a friend were standing on a hill in a clearing overlooking a field at the edge of an airstrip. Pilots practiced landings and takeoffs. One of the pilots flew a bright red plane with two sets of wings. It was a biplane, a type that was common at the time.

The pilot spotted the girls and flew down, thinking he'd give them a scare. As he zoomed in, he noticed that the taller woman was not frightened at all.

Amelia Earhart stood on top of the hill, mesmerized as she stared up at the plane shooting by overhead. She later told a friend that she was sure the little red airplane said something to her as it passed overhead. Whatever the plane whispered that day outside Toronto, it pulled her into the sky.

Shortly after that, she and her father attended another air show, this one in Long Beach, California. Her father paid $10—a steep price—so his daughter could fly for the first time. She had watched long enough. It was time for her to feel flying for herself.

Amelia Earhart said later that she was thrilled by her short flight over Long Beach. She knew before the plane landed that she would have to learn to fly.

Choosing to become a pilot was not something to be taken lightly. Lessons were very expensive. But Amelia Earhart didn't let that stop her. She went after jobs like an energetic hurricane, doing anything that would pay enough for her to save up the $1,000 she needed for lessons. This included work as a photographer, truck driver, and secretary.

Amelia Earhart would have done anything to get into the air.

To get out to the airport for her lessons, she had to take a bus to the end of the line. Then, she had to walk four miles. It was a long way, but it was worth it. At the airport, she met with her instructor, a woman named Neta Snook.

When she wasn't taking lessons with Neta Snook, Amelia Earhart read everything she could find on flying. She cut her hair short, in the style of other female pilots of the day—not that there were many of them. After splurging on a grand leather flying jacket, she slept in it for a week to give it a worn look before she wore it to the airport for her lesson.

In the early days, airplanes were not exactly reliable. Crashes were not unusual. Airfields were nothing more than cow pastures. But for Amelia Earhart, flying just felt right.

And she was excellent at flying. She couldn't get enough of it. Historians call the years from 1920 to 1929 the "Roaring 20s" because it was a time of great excitement, with so many new things happening. They might easily be called the "Soaring 20s," because Amelia Earhart took to the air like a fish to water. She was a natural.

During the next few years, she set many flying records, and her love for flying took a complete hold on her. She saved her money from working extra jobs and soon had enough to buy her own plane, a bright yellow Kinner Airster biplane she named *Canary*. Amelia and the plane were hard to miss.

On October 22, 1922, Amelia Earhart flew the Airster almost three miles high in the air, an altitude that set a world record for female pilots. On May 15, 1923, Earhart became the 16th woman in the entire world to earn a pilot's license.

Soon, people across the country began to notice this shy but determined woman. Photos of Amelia Earhart smiling after a flight and newspaper articles about her feats began to spread from California to New York. People took notice of this brave pilot who flew just as easily as other people walked.

Crossing the ocean during the 1920s usually meant sailing on a ship. This took more than a week. After a man named Charles Lindbergh flew from New York to Paris in May 1927, people wondered if a woman could do the same. Of course, their thoughts immediately turned to Amelia Earhart.

On June 17, 1928, Amelia Earhart took her place as a passenger on a plane named *Friendship*. The trip from Newfoundland, Canada, to Wales, Great Britain, took 20 hours. Amelia Earhart was an instant hero—the first woman to fly across the ocean.

When she returned to America, by boat, she was stunned at the attention. Her hero's welcome home included a ticker-tape parade in New York City, lunch with President Calvin Coolidge, and a swarm of national attention.

Everyone in America loved the brave Amelia Earhart.

But she pointed out that she did not fly the plane. She was only a passenger.

"I was just like baggage," she told reporters. "Really nothing more than a sack of potatoes."

No one listened. The public wanted to know more about this intriguing celebrity. Soon Amelia Earhart wrote a book about her flight. And she began to think about her next adventures.

She began working on secret plans to fly a plane across the Atlantic Ocean herself.

On the morning of May 20, 1932, Amelia Earhart took off alone from Harbour Grace, Newfoundland, bound for Paris, France. Quickly, she lifted the plane into the dark, rumbling clouds. As the hours passed, looking out her window from the pilot's seat, she could see that the airplane's wings were beginning to cover with ice. Icy wings are not a good thing.

The flight became bumpy and jarring, and everything in the plane shook. Always calm, Amelia Earhart realized she would never make it to Paris. She calmly landed in a pasture outside a small village in Northern Ireland, 15 hours and 2,000 miles after takeoff.

It was not a perfect flight, but she had done it. She was the first woman to fly across the Atlantic by herself. This time she had been the pilot, not a sack of potatoes.

Amelia Earhart became the most famous person in the United States! She won a gold medal for heroism from the National Geographic Society, presented to her by U.S. President Herbert Hoover. She received the Distinguished Flying Cross from the U.S. Congress and the Cross of the Knight of the Legion of Honor from the French government.

The attention and fame did not stop her from flying and setting more records. She flew from Honolulu, Hawaii, to Oakland, California. She became the first person to fly across both the Atlantic and the Pacific Oceans. After flying from Los Angeles, California, to Mexico City, Mexico, a month later, she flew from Mexico City to New York. Between 1930 and 1935, Amelia Earhart set seven women's speed and distance aviation records in a variety of aircraft.

By 1935, Amelia Earhart began to think about a flight that would set her apart from all others. She wanted to circle the world at the equator, the earth's widest point.

No one, man or woman, had ever done such a thing.

She would need a new plane. Amelia Earhart chose a Lockheed Electra 10E, the best airplane available for such a dangerous and challenging flight.

Next, she assembled a team of the most experienced pilots to help her. This team included the top navigator in the world, a man named Fred Noonan. He would join her on the flight around the world.

Who wouldn't want the chance to set a record with Amelia Earhart? But if Frank Noonan had known their fate, he might have not have been so eager to volunteer.

She would need as much expertise and advice as possible to face the many perils waiting for her and her plane. There were far more chances to crash into the vast ocean than there were to land on any of the small islands where they planned to stop and refuel.

Amelia Earhart was not afraid, though. She casually referred to dying on the flight as "popping off." It was as if it would be no more than a long sleep.

Her original plan was to fly west across the Pacific from California to Hawaii, then hop from tiny island to tiny island, one leg at a time, to

Australia, India, Africa, Florida, and then back to California. That would set a record no one would be able to touch.

The last part of the trip would be easier than the first. It was only over the Pacific Ocean that the chances of disappearing were high.

On March 17, 1937, Amelia and her crew took off from Oakland on the first leg, packed tightly into the Electra. They met some bumps and stormy weather on the way, but by long-distance flying standards, the flight was almost boring.

That changed when they tried to leave Hawaii.

As the plane lifted off, it twisted and crashed. Amelia Earhart walked away with only a few bruises, but the plane was wrecked and needed serious repair work. They called off the trip temporarily, and the plane was shipped back to California to be fixed.

Amelia Earhart came up with a new plan while she waited. This time, she would fly east around the world, though still at the equator.

The distance around the world would be the same. She would still have to cross the vast Pacific. But the winds would be better flying east.

On June 1, everything was ready. With navigator Fred Noonan directing the way, Amelia Earhart gleefully piloted the plane out of Miami amid the usual fanfare for anything she did. She was happy to watch the crowds fade as she guided the plane into the south Florida sky and headed to Central America.

From there, she crossed the Atlantic to Africa, then pointed the Electra over the Indian Ocean

Amelia Earhart with her Lockheed Electra

and eventually landed at Lae, Papua New Guinea. Hopping her way around the world, she had flown 22,000 miles in all by then. Amelia Earhart was tired but elated at the accomplishment of coming so far.

Ahead of them, she knew, the landing places would be smaller and harder to find. The distances between stops would be longer and more perilous. The easiest part of the trip was over. More than 7,000 miles of Pacific Ocean lay ahead.

At Lae, the flight was delayed a few days while Amelia Earhart recovered from a stomach bug, but no one worried. They made use of the time by stowing extra fuel.

Amelia Earhart made the decision to toss aside the parachutes they had been carrying. There would be no need for parachutes on the next part of the trip. If they went down, there was no use parachuting into the emptiness.

She also removed the radios that could broadcast long distances but did not work so well over short distances. We need the fuel more than we need these long-distance radios, she reasoned.

From Lae, Amelia Earhart and Fred Noonan planned to fly more than 2,500 miles to Howland Island, a flat dot of land between Australia and Hawaii. It was the sort of place a pilot would miss if she blinked. The distance was at the very edge of the Electra's capabilities.

Howland was no more than 20 feet higher than the waves that crashed around it. But it had a runway and was an ideal place to land.

If they could find it.

Amelia Earhart planned well, as always. A U.S. Coast Guard vessel would be standing by off Howland Island with its radios tuned into the plane. The *Itasca's* signals would help guide Amelia Earhart. But that depended on her remaining radios working.

Once they got close enough to Howland Island, they would talk to the radiomen aboard *Itascsa*. The plan was for the ship to send up smoke signals to guide Amelia Earhart and Fred Noonan in for a safe landing.

They even had emergency plans for ditching the plane if it ran out of fuel, which was a very real possibility given the distance. Amelia Earhart believed the plane's empty fuel tanks would keep it afloat and give them time to get into the life raft.

On paper, the plan was flawless. But reality is usually very different from written plans.

Amelia Earhart and Fred Noonan set out from Lae on July 2, 1937, at 12:30 p.m., heading east toward Howland. Things began to go wrong immediately. Just as they lifted from the runway, a witness said he noticed that the Electra's radio antenna seemed damaged. It was a crucial piece of equipment.

As they flew toward Howland Island, the clear night sky became clouded. Cloudy skies would make it difficult for Fred Noonan to use the stars to guide the plane. Each problem by itself was nothing to worry about, but taken together, they could mean disaster.

With a broken antenna, no long-distance radios, and no stars, they had no way to accurately guide the small plane to the dot of the island. They had no way to call for help. After hours of nervous flying, Amelia Earhart and Fred Noonan arrived at the spot where they thought Howland Island sat.

There was nothing below them but the rolling sea, empty of everything but waves.

Around that time, the radio on the *Itasca* came to life. It was Amelia Earhart. She and Fred Noonan had to be close enough for a radio transmission to work, but over the vast Pacific Ocean, a mile off course might as well be 10,000 miles. If Amelia Earhart and Fred Noonan missed the island, there was nothing but empty ocean ahead, behind, and all around.

"We must be on you," Amelia Earhart told the radio operator on the *Itasca*, "but we cannot see you. Been unable to reach you by radio. We are flying at 1,000 feet and fuel is running low."

The radio operator replied, but no one knows if Amelia Earhart heard it.

The *Itasca* fired up its oil burners and sent up clouds of thick black smoke to guide them in. Did Amelia Earhart ever see the rising plumes?

An hour after Amelia Earhart's last message, the *Itasca* set out to rescue the doomed plane. The U.S. navy joined in as well. But the searchers found nothing. Finding a small airplane and two people bobbing in the ocean was as likely as spotting a pinhead on a sidewalk from the top of a 50-story building.

Still, the search continued in all directions and covered more than 150,000 square miles. But there was no sign of Amelia Earhart or Fred Noonan or even bits of the Electra. Finally, the official search was abandoned.

Amelia Earhart and Fred Noonan were never seen or heard from again.

Amelia Earhart's disappearance was difficult for the tens of thousands of people who loved her and admired her courage. The public felt as though they had lost a dear friend. Many refused to believe she was gone. Amelia Earhart was too strong, too brave, and too resourceful simply to disappear, they thought.

After the navy abandoned its search, friends of Amelia Earhart refused to give up. They hoped that she had survived and was living on a deserted island, maybe eating coconuts and waiting for rescue. They chartered boats and other planes and searched for months, hopping from one small island to the next.

They never found any signs of Amelia Earhart or her Electra anywhere.

Amelia Earhart had a magical pull on people's imaginations. Even today, 80 years after she vanished, people are still looking for some sign of what might have happened that fateful day.

As the years passed, there were many theories, including one that the pair survived on another island for a time. But so far there have been no proven answers.

Searchers still hope to find a sign—a scrap of metal from the Electra, perhaps, or maybe a small piece of wire from the radio—that would prove that Amelia Earhart and Fred Noonan made it to land.

That would be at least some small victory.

WHAT ELSE HAPPENED IN 1937?

- There is much news about flying. Eccentric millionaire Howard Hughes sets a new speed record for flying across the country, dashing from Los Angeles, California, to Newark, New Jersey, in 7 hours, 28 minutes.

- A human-powered aircraft called the Pedaliante flies 1 kilometer near Milan, Italy.

- The German airship Hindenburg explodes in flames and disintegrates in Lakehurst, New Jersey, killing 36.

- A German Messerschmitt airplane sets a world speed record of 710 kilometers per hour.

- The first airmail letter to go around the world lands back in New York City.

NORWAY

SWEDEN

FINLAND

GERMANY

POLAND

HUNGARY

ROMANIA

RUSSIA

Yekaterinburg

1 St. Petersburg

TURKEY

1. 1901–1917
Anastasia Romanov lives
a charmed life as a
princess, the daughter of
the tsar, in St. Petersburg,
the capital of Russia.

2. July 1918
Anastasia and her family
are held captive in
Yekaterinburg, where they
are finally murdered during
the Russian Revolution.

YOU
ARE
HERE

Chapter Three

The Missing Princess

For most of her life, Anastasia Romanov
seemed charmed. Everyone loved her sunny,
mischievous personality. She had her family,
her dog, parties to attend, and people to meet.
How could her life have changed so much that
she found herself sewing jewels into her clothes
to hide them? She did this in case one day she
found herself alone and in need of money.

How did life get so bad? And how could she
have known it would get much, much worse?

As a young girl, Anastasia Romanov lived a
fairy tale life in Russia more than 100 years ago.
She wore the best clothes, lived in grand city
mansions and rolling country estates, and had
servants who cared for her every need.

Anastasia Romanov was happy and joyful. She snatched up each moment of every day as if it were a precious jewel. Everything that happened during the day was like a gift she could never get enough of. Her joy for living was contagious.

Anastasia Romanov was born on June 18, 1901, in Petrodvorets, Russia, a town near the large city of St. Petersburg. The Romanov family had ruled Russia for more than 300 years. Her father, Nicholas II, was Russia's tsar, the most powerful man in the country. His decisions affected everyone.

A young Anastasia Romanov and her older sisters (PD-US)

Her mother was known as Empress Alexandra. Anastasia had three older sisters named Olga, Tatiana, and Maria, and a younger brother named Alexei.

Nicholas II ruled over the vast, powerful country of Russia at the turn of the twentieth century. It was a shaky time for rulers to rule over anything. The world was changing.

Even though Alexei was the youngest, he was next in line to rule over Russia. Girls could not become tsars. But this fact didn't bother Anastasia Romanov in the least. She and her sisters did not exactly suffer while they were growing up. They were princesses! They lived very well.

The funny thing about Anastasia Romanov was that she would have been just as happy wearing a ragged dress and living in a hut with a leaky roof and mud floors. She would have smiled just as often had she been working in the fields as the cold Russian wind blew across the wide steppes.

She also had a strong sense of mischief and loved playing pranks on her family. One night, at a royal dinner for some important visitors, her father and mother tried hard to entertain their guests properly. Anastasia Romanov and her younger brother had a better idea. They crept quietly under the table and began barking like hungry puppies. They even pinched the startled diners, who pretended not to notice the chaos at their feet.

Anastasia Romanov's parents were angry! Lucky for her, they could never stay angry for long. Anastasia Romanov was their favorite. Her frustrated parents loved her dearly. Her family even gave her a nickname, which she did everything she could to live up to: "Schwibsik," which means "Imp."

Anastasia Romanov had her own sense of style. She was short for her age and had long, strawberry blonde hair and bright blue eyes. Once, as a joke, Anastasia Romanov braided her hair with long ribbons of many different colors. She looked silly, as if she was wearing a colorful flag woven into her hair.

The Russian people adored the tsar and his family so much, though. Soon, almost every young girl in St. Petersburg was braiding her hair with long, colored ribbons.

Anastasia Romanov was an imp! Whether she and her family were attending an opera by Rimsky-Korsakov or a performance by the world-famous Bolshoi Ballet, she was determined to be true to her outrageous self.

One time, she caused a stir as she sat next to her mother at the theater. In those days, women and girls wore white linen gloves on their hands when they traveled out of the house. Anastasia Romanov didn't think it was necessary to remove her gloves before eating chocolate from a decorated red box.

What a mess! But Anastasia did not care. She smiled to herself and shoveled more bits of melting chocolate into her mouth while her gloves turned brown and sticky, as did her face.

Anastasia Romanov's charmed life of dinner parties, theater, and hair ribbons was not destined to last forever. As she grew older, dark clouds began to form on the horizon of her days.

At first, there were only small signs of trouble. Grumbling rumors spread that some people were not happy with Tsar Nicholas II. These rumors passed, and Anastasia Romanov wasn't concerned. However, even a gentle rain can turn into a devastating hurricane.

One sure sign that things were changing was the presence of the weird and mysterious Grigory Rasputin. Rasputin was a wandering monk who many considered a holy man with special powers. Anastasia Romanov's parents thought he was pretty special.

Rasputin turned people's heads wherever he went. First of all, he was more than 6 feet 6 inches tall, so he wasn't hard to miss. He dressed in long, flowing robes. His thin face was mostly hidden by a long, dark beard.

But it was Rasputin's eyes that made people catch their breaths and try to look away—most people failed. It was as if the giant man had a magnetic pull no one could resist. When Rasputin stared at someone, they froze.

Both Nicholas II and Alexandra thought that Rasputin had the answers to their problems. The empress believed that Rasputin had secret powers.

Anastasia Romanov's brother, Alexei, had a serious medical condition. It caused his parents a great deal of worry and many sleepless nights. If Alexei got even the tiniest scratch, it would take a very long time to stop bleeding. It was so bad that even a scraped knee could kill him.

Rasputin visited Alexei when he was very sick in bed from a bad bruise. Rasputin sent the doctors away and chanted over the boy. Soon Alexei appeared to be better. After that, Rasputin became a favorite with the entire Romanov family.

Anastasia Romanov and her sisters grew very fond of Rasputin, who spent a lot of time with the royal family. Rasputin spoke in his low, soothing way to the girls and told them wonderful stories that kept them on the edges of their chairs.

Anastasia later told a friend that Rasputin was her "only true friend."

Rasputin

Rasputin was not everyone's friend, though. Many of the people who worked with Tsar Nicholas were jealous of Rasputin's influence over the tsar and the empress. They tried to convince Nicholas II and Alexandra that he was bad news. Many thought that Rasputin was the reason that the rumors about the tsar and his weak position were growing stronger. They couldn't understand why the tsar and his family wanted to spend so much time with this strange person.

But what could they do? How could they come between the Romanov family and their trusted friend?

One night in the winter of 1915, a group of men decided Rasputin was becoming too friendly with the tsar. They invited Rasputin to a quiet dinner. The wine and food they gave him was laced with cyanide, a poison that immediately kills anyone who swallows it.

Much to the surprise of the men who had invited him to dinner, Rasputin kept talking. He asked for more pastries and wine. Cyanide did not seem to bother Rasputin at all.

The men grew desperate. They wanted Rasputin dead! While Rasputin was still eating at the table, one of them walked up behind him and shot him in the head. Rasputin fell to the ground, and they all cheered with relief.

However, when one of the men checked on him, Rasputin sat up and opened his eyes. How could a body with no pulse, who'd been poisoned and shot, still survive? Perhaps the man did have mysterious powers.

The men beat Rasputin, tied him up, and threw him into a freezing river. When his body was later dragged from the river, his arm had managed to escape the rope. Was Rasputin alive when he was tossed in the water? Had he survived the poison, the shooting, and the beating? Powerful men in the city prevented the police from making a full investigation.

It was a violent ending that signaled violent things to come. The world was changing, and not in a good way for Anastasia Romanov and her family. For her, the death of Rasputin, a man who was so close to the family, was the beginning of the end. Nothing in her fairy tale life would ever be the same.

For the first time in her life, Anastasia Romanov became frightened.

World War I had begun in 1914, which meant Tsar Nicholas II had to lead the Russian troops into battle. The whole family missed him. Laughter became less frequent in the Romanov home.

When Tsar Nicholas II returned home from the front, he found that the Russian people no longer wanted a tsar. Instead, they wanted to rule themselves. They wanted independence.

While independence is a great thing for people to strive for, there are always groups waiting to take advantage of chaos in a country. Those groups want to steal some power for themselves.

Revolutions are always violent.

Soon, the Romanov family's grand, elegant world of palaces and large country estates began to shrink. The tsar lost much of his power. Instead of living anywhere they wanted in Russia, the Romanovs were told where to go by a new group of men who had taken control of the country. These men called themselves Bolsheviks.

At first, the family was ordered to stay in the Alexander Palace in St. Petersburg, which was Anastasia Romanov's favorite place. But this time, soldiers surrounded them and watched their every move.

Anastasia felt more like a prisoner than a princess. In a letter to a friend, she wrote, "Goodbye and don't forget us." Did she suspect that her family was in deep trouble?

Nicholas II begged the men holding them captive to allow his family to move to England, where they would be safe. No one listened. The tsar had no power. His pleas fell on deaf ears. Instead of Britain, the tsar and his family were forced to move from the luxurious Alexander Palace to a small, isolated town called Tobolsk, 1,200 miles way.

There, they were treated even more like prisoners. They were allowed to take only short walks outside. Otherwise, they were trapped inside like criminals in jail. The guards stared at them with hatred in their eyes. This was the family that had lived in luxury while people went hungry on the streets of St. Petersburg, the guards thought. This family is only getting what it has always deserved.

Anastasia Romanov tried to keep up everyone's spirits by putting on plays and reading exciting stories aloud. But everyone was frightened about what might come next in their lives.

The Romanov sisters came up with the idea of sewing their jewels into their dresses. Why would they do this? If they ever managed to escape, they'd need money to survive. Anastasia Romanov seemed to have known something bad was about to happen.

The new rulers of Russia decided that the Romanovs should be moved again, to a city named Yekaterinburg. It would be their final move.

The Romanov family, two years before their murders

The last time anyone other than the rough Russian guards saw them, the Romanov sisters and their young brother were lugging their heavy suitcase through the muddy streets, whispering among themselves. In Yekaterinburg, Anastasia Romanov and her sisters lived in a cramped two-bedroom apartment and slept on mattresses on the floor.

The windows of the apartment were painted over. The family was allowed outside for only a few minutes a day. The guards taunted them and rarely left them alone.

On July 17, 1918, the soldiers ordered Anastasia Romanov and her family into the damp, dark cellar of the house. They were told to sit on wooden chairs arranged in a row. Her parents were asked to sit and join them. Was this a meeting? Were they going to be forced to move again?

A few moments later, a group of guards rushed into the basement and fired their rifles at the shocked Romanovs. The horrible noise of guns and screaming lasted only a few minutes.

When it was over, Tsar Nicholas II, the Empress Alexandra, and their children were dead.

What happened next in the smoke-filled basement has been the source of arguments for 100 years.

As the smoke from the gunfire cleared, the soldiers quickly covered the bodies of the tsar and his family and carried them away. The bodies were buried in a secret place. There could be no evidence of the grisly killings.

The scene in the basement was so chaotic that no one who was there could remember exactly what happened. Were all members of the family killed? Were any of them left alive? Confusion and secrecy combined to bury the facts in history.

Had Anastasia Romanov somehow escaped? Remember the jewels that the sisters had sewn into their dresses and carried with them? Had the hidden jewels stopped the bullets? Some people thought so. They began to believe that Anastasia only pretended to be dead and was later helped by a sympathetic soldier to escape. Many who had loved her hoped that story was true.

Almost two years after the grim scene in the basement in Yekaterinburg, a shabbily dressed young woman appeared in Berlin, Germany. It was nearly 2,000 miles away from Yekaterinburg. The woman was upset and asked passing strangers for help. She told them she was Anastasia. For years, people believed the story.

The mysterious young woman in Berlin was not the only one to claim she was Anastasia. More than 30 others came forward through the decades claiming that they, too, were Anastasia.

In 1991, when the graves of the tsar and his family were excavated, searchers found the bodies of the tsar, his wife, and three of the children. But two children were missing. Who? Where were they? What had happened to them? Could they have survived? These missing bodies spurred even more speculation that Anastasia Romanov had escaped death.

In 2007, a second grave was discovered. There, researchers found the two missing bodies. Scientists used DNA tests to determine that these bodies belonged to the Romanov son, Alexei, and a female relative. This means that the entire family, including Anastasia, was accounted for.

That, some said, was the end of the story.

WHAT ELSE HAPPENED IN 1918?

- On April 20, Manfred von Richthofen, the famous "Red Baron," shoots down his 79th and 80th enemy airplanes. They are the last shot down by the most feared fighter pilot of WWI. The German pilot was shot down and killed the next day.

- The U.S. Postal Service issues its first airmail stamps, charging 24 cents to deliver a letter between New York City and Washington, DC.

- The first Tarzan movie makes its debut in January.

- Margaret Owen sits down at a non-electric typewriter and sets a new world typing record of 170 words in one minute.

- On May 21, the U.S. House of Representatives passes a new law allowing women to vote. The law fails in the Senate, though. It takes two more years for an amendment to the constitution to pass, finally giving women the right to vote.

- On the morning of June 15, residents of northern Pennsylvania are surprised to wake and see it is snowing. More than 15 inches fall before the end of the day.

- During the week of October 31, a virulent epidemic of the Spanish flu kills more than 21,000 people in the United States. The worldwide epidemic infects more than 500 million people before it ends in 1920.

- In December, authorities in New York City introduce the world's first three-color traffic light. Drivers in New York have been honking ever since.

Venezuela

Colombia

Guyana

Suriname

French Guiana

Ecuador

B r a z i l

Peru

Bolivia

2 Cuiabá

Chile

Paraguay

1

Rio de Janeiro

Argentina

Uruguay

1. 1925
Percy Fawcett arrives in Rio de Janeiro to embark on a journey into the wilds of Brazil in search of what he called the Lost City of Z.

2. 1925
Cuiabá is the last known sighting of Percy Fawcett and his two traveling companions.

YOU ARE HERE

N
E
S
W

Chapter Four

Swallowed by the Amazon

Percy Fawcett had heard the stories about a lost city hidden in the thick, dangerous Amazon rainforest, a place some called El Dorado. The long trip to get there had a well-deserved reputation for killing uninvited explorers.

He knew that, since ancient times, thousands of men had looked for El Dorado and its piles of gold. They had never found it. Percy Fawcett knew that many of those men died painful deaths.

Some had been shot with poison arrows. Some had been torn apart by wild jaguars or crushed by huge snakes. Others had been trapped in the steamy, impenetrable jungle and starved to death. Some had gone stark raving crazy.

It seemed from the stories Percy Fawcett heard, every expedition that set out to find this golden kingdom ended in disaster.

On one expedition, a Spanish conquistador had led 4,000 men to their deaths while searching for El Dorado. Before they died, most of the lost and frantic men ate the leather from their shoes. When they ran out of shoes, some began to eat the dead.

Did these stories stop Percy Fawcett from trying to find the mythical city in 1925? Absolutely not.

The lost city was known to have fine buildings, wide, paved streets, and civilized inhabitants. Percy Fawcett had also heard there was so much gold in this lost city that residents ground it into powder and blew it onto their bodies through hollow canes in joyful displays of their riches. He had visions of gold-covered residents walking the wide city streets, gathering in the center of the city where a large, fabulous pyramid stood as the center of business.

The thought of being the first man to discover the lost city and its gold-covered inhabitants was worth every sacrifice, he thought. However, Percy Fawcett was not motived by gold. He was driven by adventure and a thirst for knowledge. How did the city form? What were the people like?

The city and its gold were protected by a vast expanse of land, the Amazon rainforest.

And that was the challenge Percy Fawcett couldn't resist—the chance to prove himself a better explorer than anyone. He would survive the rainforest on his way to El Dorado, or the Lost City of Z, as he referred to it. Somewhere in the Amazon rainforest, the world's largest and most dangerous jungle, was the prize he felt destined to find.

Percy Fawcett knew the horrors of the Amazon rainforest as well as any man because he had explored there for years. He had made six trips into the deadly jungle! He knew what lay ahead of him, should he venture to find the Lost Land of Z.

The Amazon River Basin is home to the largest rainforest on Earth. The basin covers about 40 percent of South America. This is roughly the same size as the 48 lower United States. It includes parts of nine South American countries: Brazil, Bolivia, Peru, Ecuador, Colombia, Venezuela, Guyana, Suriname, and French Guiana.

Imagine walking from New York City to Pittsburgh, Pennsylvania, hacking through thick trees, tripping over meandering vines in 100-degree heat. Imagine mosquitoes and killer animals watching you day and night. Imagine reaching Pittsburgh and realizing you aren't even close to the end of the trail. That's what it was like to take a trip into the Amazon rainforest.

On his trips into the Amazon, Percy Fawcett learned a lot. Most people who knew what he knew would never have made it back from the rainforest.

Percy Fawcett knew about the piranha that swam in the lakes and rivers of the Amazon. He was personally familiar with the razor-sharp teeth of these vicious little fish. Piranhas are like miniature sharks that swim in large, deadly packs. When angry or upset, the piranha can tear the flesh from a person's leg in seconds—and piranhas seem angry and upset all the time.

Percy Fawcett had heard plenty of stories about schools of piranha devouring bodies in less than a minute. They left nothing but bones to sink to the murky bottom.

He was also familiar with the anacondas of the Amazon. Percy Fawcett knew that these giant snakes were thicker than telephone poles and could crush a man in the blink of an eye. An anaconda could silently slither up to a sleeping man, wrap its giant trunk around its victim, and squeeze tightly until the person suffocated. An anaconda might even keep squeezing until the body popped.

Percy Fawcett had heard stories about a hungry anaconda swallowing a deer whole.

On one of his expeditions to the Amazon rainforest, Percy Fawcett paddled his canoe over what he thought was a fallen tree just below the surface of the slow-moving river.

But the sunken tree seemed to come alive. It moved ever so slowly toward the canoe. Percy Fawcett, a man who never lost his cool, gasped when he saw that the giant snake was nearly 60 feet long.

Percy Fawcett quickly pulled a rifle from behind his seat in the canoe and shot the anaconda. He paddled his canoe alongside the enormous snake that floated on the surface of the water. He pulled a knife from his pack, thinking he would take a slice of the anaconda's thick skin to send to London to be studied by scientists.

The snake had other ideas.

When Percy Fawcett's knife cut into the anaconda's thick skin, the water erupted in a froth, and the snake turned toward the crew. It was still alive and very upset at being shot and sliced.

Percy Fawcett and his men barely made it to the safety of the shore. They turned to watch where the anaconda sunk back into the river. No one slept that night.

Percy Fawcett made other mysterious discoveries during his journeys. He saw a small, cat-like dog the size of a foxhound and a giant apazauca spider that had bitten and killed a number of locals.

Water is everywhere in the Amazon. That is why the trees and vegetation grow so thick and lush. But water is not always a good thing.

Water provides shelter for things such as 6-foot-long electric eels, which have long, flat, ugly faces with eyes resting right on top of their lips. These strange creatures are like high-voltage wires that can breathe and swim. They can send a shock through the water to kill a fish without even touching it.

A person wading in water where an electric eel was swimming could be stunned, paralyzed, and have sunk to the bottom before ever knowing what happened.

The Amazon is also home to ants that can attack a person and tear their clothes and backpack to shreds in a minute or two. There are ticks and blood-sucking leeches that attach themselves to any bare spots of skin to feast on flesh and blood.

Then there are millipedes. These thick, wooly torpedoes of danger shoot poisonous cyanide into the backsides of anyone unsuspecting enough to sit in the wrong place.

How about tiny flying bugs no bigger than gnats that swarm so thickly they can choke you? Percy Fawcett always brought nets to attach to the broad-brimmed hat he always wore. It was clumsy and looked quite odd but it kept the bugs from his face and from getting caught in his thick beard.

The bugs' bites were irritating enough, to be sure. But scientists would learn later that a bite on the arm from one of these pests would send tiny parasites into a victim's blood. Eventually, the parasites would make their way to a person's brain, where they would eat until the person went insane.

Percy Fawcett knew an Amazonian explorer who died from madness 20 years after his trip because of those bug bites.

Those are just the things that nature tosses at an unprepared explorer. There are also human dangers. Percy Fawcett was attacked and shot at many times, barely escaping with his life. In the early twentieth century, some of the people who lived in the Amazon did not take kindly to explorers.

People often asked him about the dangers. What dangers? He might reply. Yawn. Percy Fawcett was not concerned about danger.

Percy Fawcett was an extraordinarily strong man. He was fit and lean and wiry. He could walk for days without food and very little rest. It was as if he was made for the Amazon and all it could throw at an explorer. It was if he was meant to find the Lost City of Z.

In January 1925, he prepared for his next trip to the Amazon, the journey he was certain would lead him to the Lost City of Z.

Percy Fawcett knew that traveling in a big group would slow him down. It takes time to patch an arrow wound or fix ribs broken by an anaconda attack or to bandage flesh from a calf muscle torn by swarming piranha. It takes even more time to bury a dead body.

The fewer the people on the trip, the fewer delays, he reasoned. He would bring only his son, Jack, and Jack's best friend, a young man named Raleigh Rimell. With only three people, things would be much more efficient.

Jack Fawcett was only 21. He trained for the strains of the trip for months. Raleigh Rimell did the same. They were both in top physical form, and they were just as obsessed with finding the Lost City of Z as Percy Fawcett.

On this trip, Percy Fawcett decided that he would avoid time-consuming river trips. These often took him miles off course. For this trip, he would take a direct route over land.

He would find trails carved out by indigenous peoples who had lived there for centuries or simply hack straight through the thick forest with sharp machetes to make his path. It would be much harder, but if it worked, his plan would save months of time.

He knew, though, that things would not be easy. Once inside the rainforest, they would rarely see the sun. The air would be so thick, hot, and wet that breathing would be difficult, like trying to breathe through a wet towel. The slightest effort would produce rivers of perspiration that would attract insects and leeches.

There would be little rest until they reached the Lost City of Z.

Very few people doubted that Percy Fawcett would be the man to find the Lost City of Z. A few of his friends even dared to say that Percy Fawcett was immune to death—Percy Fawcett could out-hike and out-explore any man on Earth.

After loading up on mosquito netting, canned food, machetes, and other provisions, Percy Fawcett was ready. He and his two companions set sail from New York City. By then, newspapers were following the progress of his planning. People all around the world were convinced he'd succeed in finding the Lost City of Z. Photographs of Percy Fawcett showed him smiling and ready for what looked like a perfect adventure. Percy Fawcett looked like a swashbuckling adventurer.

"We shall return," Fawcett said to reporters just before the ship threw off its lines and headed seaward. "And we shall bring back what we seek."

As the skyline dropped below the horizon, he stood at the rail and took a long, satisfying breath. Soon, he would be back where he belonged, in the thick jungle between Peru and Bolivia. He would be back in the merciless Amazon. He would be home.

Percy Fawcett was convinced that the Lost City of Z was lurking somewhere in the unexplored Mato Grosso region of Brazil. He was going to find it.

Percy Fawcett left behind instructions saying that if the expedition did not return, no one should go looking for them. If they met with unfortunate events, anyone trying to rescue them would meet the same fate.

He refused to reveal to newspaper reporters or anyone else the route he planned to take. He did not want anyone following him.

Percy Fawcett (PD-US)

After landing in Rio de Janeiro, the Fawcetts and Raleigh Rimell trekked inland to the remote outpost of Cuiabá. Percy Fawcett hired two guides to help them get started and bought two horses, eight mules, and two dogs. The easiest part of the trip was over.

Percy Fawcett had warned his son and Raleigh Rimell about the heat, the piranhas, the anacondas, and the dozens of other frightful things that might attack. But he had not warned them enough about the insects. Mosquitoes attacked them in swarms all day long. Blood-sucking gnats made sleep all but impossible. Raleigh Rimell's foot swelled enormously from tick bites. Things were starting to go wrong.

Still, Percy Fawcett pushed hard. For the first two weeks, the three explorers kept a pace of 10 to 15 miles a day—normal distances if you're walking in a city, but pretty impressive for the Amazon.

On May 29, the team reached a place nicknamed "Dead Horse Camp." Years earlier, Percy Fawcett had been forced to shoot his exhausted horse at the spot. He asked the two guides to unload their gear and then he sent them back to Cuiabá. Before the guides left, Percy Fawcett wrote a letter for them to deliver to his wife, Nina, Jack's mother.

"Jack is well and fit and getting stronger every day," he wrote. "You need have no fear of any failure."

The guides were the last people to see the three intrepid explorers alive.

At first, because Percy Fawcett had said he wanted no one to follow them, no one did. No one was worried. Percy Fawcett can take care of himself, everyone said. It was only after two years had gone by that people started to worry.

By 1927, the same newspapers that had written that Percy Fawcett was invincible began asking where he was. Rumors began circulating that Percy Fawcett might be dead. And because no one could go into the forbidding Amazon to find out what actually happened, even more rumors began spreading faster than a piranha attack.

One rumor claimed Percy Fawcett was alive and well and living alone in the jungle. Another reported that all three men were being held prisoner by Indians. Another man reported that Percy Fawcett had become chief of a tribe of cannibals.

In 1928, three years after Percy Fawcett left New York harbor, an expedition set off into the Amazon to try to learn what had happened to

Percy and Jack Fawcett and Raleigh Rimell. Expedition leaders even hoped they might be able to rescue the three if they were being held hostage. The supposed rescuers emerged from the jungle months later, convinced the three men had perished. Still, they had found no bodies.

In the years since that first 1928 expedition, more than 13 separate trips have been made to discover what happened to Percy Fawcett. More than 100 people have died trying to find the answer.

The dangers and the mystery of the Amazon have not changed or weakened since Percy Fawcett made his final trip in 1925.

As recently as 1996, a team led by a wealthy businessman looking for clues to what happened to Percy Fawcett was captured by Amazonian Indians and held for ransom. They escaped with their lives only after giving up $30,000 worth of equipment.

There are still no definite answers, only guesses about what happened. The Amazon rarely gives up its secrets.

WHAT ELSE HAPPENED IN 1925?

- Dogsleds carrying life-saving serum to stop a raging diphtheria epidemic reach Nome, Alaska, after a harrowing journey of 674 miles from Nenana. The event is commemorated each year with the Iditarod Trail Sled Dog Race.

- In March, Tennessee passes a law making it illegal to teach the theory of evolution in schools. In July, teacher John T. Scopes is found guilty of breaking the new law and fined $100 in a trial that draws national attention.

- America's first motel opens in San Luis Obispo, California.

- Nellie Tayloe Ross becomes the first female governor elected in the United States when she takes office in Wyoming.

- Richard G. Drew invents Scotch tape.

- Calvin Coolidge becomes the first president of the United States to have his inauguration broadcast on the radio.

- Frank Heath, a retired soldier, begins a two-year journey to visit all 48 states on horseback when he leaves Washington, DC, with his horse, Gypsy Queen. They finish the nearly 12,000-mile journey on November 4, 1927.

- More than 40,000 members of the Ku Klux Klan march down Pennsylvania Avenue in Washington, DC, on August 8, showing it was the most popular fraternal organization in the country.

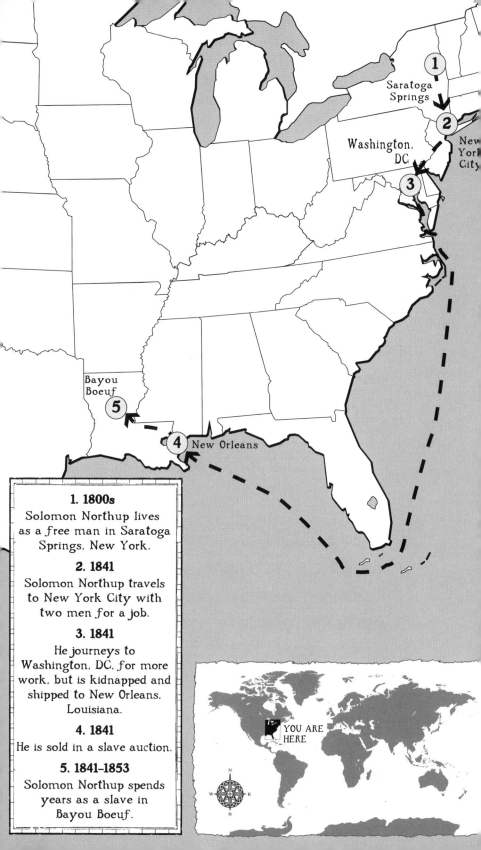

Saratoga
Springs

①

②

New
York
City

Washington,
DC

③

Bayou
Boeuf

⑤

④ New Orleans

1. 1800s
Solomon Northup lives
as a free man in Saratoga
Springs, New York.

2. 1841
Solomon Northup travels
to New York City with
two men for a job.

3. 1841
He journeys to
Washington, DC, for more
work, but is kidnapped and
shipped to New Orleans,
Louisiana.

4. 1841
He is sold in a slave auction.

5. 1841–1853
Solomon Northup spends
years as a slave in
Bayou Boeuf.

YOU ARE
HERE

N
W   E
S

Chapter Five
Solomon Northup

Solomon Northup's fingers danced across the strings of his worn fiddle as he looked out over the crowd of young people dancing like dervishes in the barn. He smiled. Solomon Northup took great pride in his musical talent. For good reason. He could make his fiddle sing.

No one else in the towns around Saratoga Springs, New York, could play as well as Solomon Northup. That's why there was no shortage of invitations for Solomon Northup to play at weddings, dances, and parties all around the area.

The sweet music he made was a comfort to everyone, including Solomon Northup himself.

He smiled again when he thought of his wife, Anne. She was such a good cook that local inns and taverns fought for her services. When Anne Northup was cooking, people came to dinner and paid well for it.

Still, life was not a dance for Solomon Northup, Anne, and their three children. Money was in short supply.

Solomon Northup tended crops on area farms and worked as a carpenter. People said Solomon Northup could build just about anything. He helped dig the Champlain Canal through the mountains of upstate New York. Later, he worked with crews that used the Champlain Canal to bring logs down from the forests near the towns of Troy and Utica.

Times were hard and money was scarce.

Solomon Northup was an African American. He had to face the constant worry of knowing that many of his neighbors looked down on him. Some even hated him, just because of the color of his skin.

The early 1800s was a time in the United States when slavery was legal in the Southern states though not in the Northern states. From the fifteenth to the nineteenth centuries, millions of Africans were kidnapped in their native lands and brought to America in chains. If they survived, which many did not, they were treated horribly. They were whipped and forced to work long, hard hours for no money.

Slaves were considered pieces of property that were bought and traded like horses or oxen.

Solomon Northup was a free man. Most people liked him and were happy to have him as a neighbor. But there was always the worry that someone would decide to hate him because of the color of his skin. Solomon Northup rarely passed a day when he did not think how lucky he was to live free in the northern town of Saratoga Springs.

One sunny afternoon at a grand hotel in Saratoga Springs, he saw two slaves with their Southern owner. The unsmiling slaves attended to their owner's needs and kept silent. Solomon Northup talked quietly with the slaves when he had a chance and asked why they didn't run away.

The answer came quickly, in a fearful whisper. If they were caught, they would be beaten and maybe even killed, the slaves told him.

Life was complicated for a slave. Solomon Northup was relieved he didn't have to live that life. Little did he know how much his fortune would change.

Solomon Northup was always on the lookout for jobs. In 1841, when he was 32 years old, a rare chance to make a lot of fast money appeared out of nowhere. Two men approached him as he walked down the main street of Saratoga Springs. The men told him they had heard he was a fine fiddler whose lively music brought many people to local dances.

Solomon Northup was a trusting and optimistic man. He liked people and wanted to think the best of everyone.

The two men told him they were from a traveling circus that had a fine group of musicians. They needed a fiddler. If Solomon Northup agreed, they would arrange for a job with the traveling circus for a few performances in New York City.

The problem, they told him, is that we have to get there quickly.

Come with us, they said. The money will be better than what you make around here.

New York City was nearly 180 miles from Saratoga Springs, which in those days meant some hard traveling. Travelers journeyed by train and horse-drawn wagon, and the trip took more than a day.

Still, Solomon Northup accepted the offer quickly. He never turned down good money to do some fiddling. Thinking he'd be back in a few days, he did not even tell Anne where he was going. He'd surprise her with a big stack of dollar bills when he returned, he thought.

He joined the men on the trip to New York City.

As promised, the two days in New York City playing his fiddle were filled with fun and laughter, and the men paid Solomon Northup well. As he prepared to head back home, they made another offer. Why not come along with us for a few more performances in Washington, DC?

The men said to Solomon Northup, we'll pay you even more money. We'll buy you a train ticket back to Saratoga Springs.

They were setting a trap, but the trusting Solomon Northup did not see that.

Caught up in the excitement and lured by the promise of more money, Solomon Northup accepted quickly. He did not think about the fact that in Washington, DC, slavery was legal.

When the three men reached the nation's capital, Solomon Northup joined his two new friends for a night of joyful celebration. The men encouraged Solomon Northup to eat and drink. They fed him and filled his glass frequently as the hours passed.

As the night moved on, Solomon Northup began feeling sick. His head spun and his stomach turned inside out. Then things went black.

When Solomon Northup awoke, he sat in a dark, dank room, unsure of where he was. His head was in a thick fog, and his two new friends were gone. So was the money that had been given him. But that was not the worst of it. When he tried to stand, he was pulled back to the muddy ground. His hands and legs were in chains.

Solomon Northup had been so happy the day before, buzzing with the excitement of a high-paying job. He did not realize that, in 1841, Washington, DC, had one of the largest slave markets in the country. He did not realize that the demand for more and more slaves to work in the South was high.

Overnight, his life had changed forever. Solomon Northup, with the shackles on his ankles digging into his skin, was about to begin a new life as a slave.

As the light of the new day began to filter slowly into his cell, Solomon Northup looked around. Other stunned victims sat around him on the dirt floor of the cell. Some whimpered, others cried silently, their heads bobbing with each painful sob.

They had all been kidnapped, and they all were about to begin a journey south. There, they would become something less than human beings.

The captives sat in the mud of the cell, not knowing they were now the property of a man named James Burch. This trader in human flesh was known for his cruelty.

Solomon Northup stood as much as the chains would let him and turned to a man who appeared to be in control.

"There has been a mistake," he told the man. "I am a free man, from Saratoga Springs in New York. I cannot be held here against my will. I demand that you set me free. My family will be asking where I am."

The man scoffed and shoved Solomon Northup to the ground. Then, he reached to a nearby wall and unhooked a long leather whip. It unrolled into a menacing weapon when the man flicked his wrist.

He turned to Solomon Northup and flailed at him with the whip, whirring and snapping it in the air. Solomon Northup's head reeled as the whip tore the shirt from his back. The skin beneath was soon tattered in shreds.

"You are my property now," the man said. "If you mention this again, I will kill you."

Shaken, Solomon Northup was led into a larger cell that held even more desperate people. No one knew what was about to happen or where they were going. No one had a good feeling about the situation. As they sat waiting, the man who had beaten Solomon Northup came into the cell and walked up to him.

"No one will be looking for you from now on," he said with a grimace. He told Solomon Northup that his papers now showed that he was a slave, property of James Burch. From that moment on, Solomon Northup was known as Platt, and any record of a free man named Solomon Northup being held in a cell in Washington, DC, was erased.

It would be impossible for anyone to find him.

The frightened people in the dank holding cell were brought to a ship docked on the nearby Potomac River. Chained below the deck, for the next two weeks they saw little light and were given hardly any food.

They knew they were heading south. As the days slowly passed, the heat and humidity grew worse. The air in their small quarters below deck became more stale and rancid.

Finally, the winds dropped and the ship slowed and docked. The strained, exhausted men and women were unchained and brought up into the harsh sunlight at the dockside. Solomon Northup looked around.

He was in New Orleans, Louisiana, and was about to be offered for sale at his first slave auction. Like a prized racehorse, he was paraded in front of interested buyers and sold to the highest bidder—a man named William Prince Ford. A Baptist preacher, William Prince Ford ran a small farm on Bayou Boeuf on the Red River in northern Louisiana. He also owned a small lumber mill.

Soon, Solomon Northup was hard at work. He was shocked and numb over what had happened to him, but hopeful he would soon be free to go home. He had no choice but to work as hard as he could.

Using what he had learned from his lumber work in Saratoga Springs, he soon began to help

William Prince Ford with his small lumber mill. Solomon Northup showed him how to build rafts from the pine trees they cut. He showed his owner how to tie the fallen trees together and float them down the narrow Indian Creek to market, where they sold quickly and at a profit.

Solomon Northup also used his skills to build a mill on the banks of Indian Creek. William Prince Ford appreciated Solomon Northup and thought himself lucky to own such a slave.

Despite Solomon Northup's help, William Prince Ford's farm lost money. The preacher soon had more debt than he could manage. He was forced to sell Solomon Northup to a hot-tempered man named John Tibeats.

This mean and spiteful man was disliked even by the local farmers. It took very little time for John Tibeats to hate the polite and accommodating Solomon Northup.

Unlike most other slaves, Solomon Northup refused to cower when John Tibeats ordered him to cut lumber or dig a hole. When he spoke, Solomon Northup looked people directly in their eyes.

He did not look down and mumble as if he was afraid. He spoke clearly and forcefully.

This did not go over well with John Tibeats, a bully who enjoyed making slaves cower.

Soon, Solomon Northup and John Tibeats began fighting. Twice, other slaves had to pull Solomon Northup from John Tibeats. A fighting slave was not welcome in Louisiana or anywhere else. Fighting an owner was an invitation to be killed.

But Solomon Northup was not afraid. During one fight with John Tibeats, Solomon Northup beat the mean owner "until my right arm ached."

During another fight, Solomon Northup had to defend himself from his owner with a hatchet. After that, John Tibeats had had enough. He announced he would kill Solomon Northup for his arrogance.

Solomon Northup ran as fast as he could into a nearby swamp. John Tibeats set a pack of dogs after him. Knowing what his fate would be if John Tibeats caught him, Solomon Northup hid in the reeds and undergrowth of the swamp. Mosquitos covered him. Leeches attached themselves to his bare legs. He had to avoid poisonous water moccasins and alligators.

As he listened to the sounds of the hounds that were tracking him, Solomon Northup slowly made his way back to the farm of William Prince Ford. There, he was able to rest until he could be sold again.

Though he was saved from John Tibeats, things would not get better. Life rarely did when one was a slave.

Solomon Northup soon found himself working on a cotton and sugar plantation owned by a man named Edwin Epps. He was like the devil personified, an evil man who enjoyed torturing his slaves. He took great pleasure in watching them suffer.

Solomon Northup realized that Edwin Epps was not a man he should fight. He knew from the moment he watched Edwin Epps whip a slave that fighting was an invitation to a slow and painful death.

Solomon Northup wanted more than anything to live. He wanted to return to Saratoga Springs and see his wife and three children. Solomon Northup wanted his freedom back.

Edwin Epps was vicious. He set daily amounts of cotton to be picked by each of his slaves. If they did not meet these goals, the slaves were whipped. Solomon Northup heard the screams when he awoke every morning. He often heard the same mournful sounds when he went to sleep.

In the slave quarters where he lived, the slaves were crammed into tiny rooms. Sometimes, they slept on the muddy ground without blankets. Discomfort and despair were a way of life.

Life on the plantation was torture for Solomon Northup. He survived nearly 10 years working for Edwin Epps. He did this by working hard, keeping silent, and hoping his chance for freedom would someday arrive.

Solomon Northup lived on a weekly supply of rotten meat, cornmeal, and a small bit of flour. He had to use it sparingly to make it last.

The food was barely enough to keep him alive. He ate a measly breakfast each morning as the sun rose, then went to work in the broiling heat, all day long.

Overseers on horseback, equipped with whips, watched closely. They consistently threatened to flog anyone they thought wasn't working hard enough. At the end of the day, the slaves were marched back to their quarters to eat a small meal and try to sleep. The next day, they did the same thing all over again.

The work never ended. It was pure misery.

The years passed slowly, and only the fading hope of freedom kept Solomon Northup from despair.

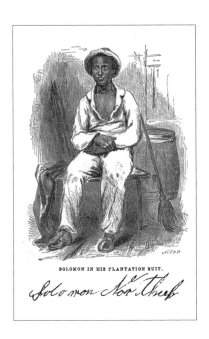

SOLOMON IN HIS PLANTATION SUIT.

A sketch of Solomon Northup by Frederick M. Coffin (engraved by Nathaniel Orr) from the autobiography, *Twelve Years a Slave*

Then something wonderful happened.

Solomon Northup was ordered to help build a new shed on the plantation. One day, he began a conversation with a carpenter who had been brought in to supervise. The man was a Canadian and, more importantly, he was angry about slavery.

The carpenter was surprised that such a horrid practice was allowed. During the days, as he worked alongside Solomon Northup, he talked about how much he hated slavery. The Canadian carpenter's name was Samuel Bass, and he would become Solomon Northup's savior.

After a few days of working together, Solomon Northup gathered his courage and told Samuel Bass his story, hoping that Samuel Bass would not run to Edwin Epps. If he did that, Edwin Epps would most certainly kill Solomon Northup—slowly and painfully.

Instead, Samuel Bass agreed to help. He began writing letters to Solomon Northup's friends in New York. Solomon is alive, he wrote, and he needs your help. Samuel Bass took a risk in doing this. Edwin Epps and his neighbors would not take kindly to anyone helping a slave.

Solomon Northup had been known as Platt for a long time. Edwin Epps had papers saying he was the rightful owner. Legally, he had bought Platt fairly and owned him outright. Things moved slowly. There were many complications.

Four months after Solomon Northup quietly told Samuel Bass his story, the news reached the right ears and someone with power took up the case.

On January 4, 1853, under the threat of a lawsuit, a very angry Edwin Epps set Solomon Northup free. It had been 12 years since Solomon had agreed to what he thought was a three-day job playing music with the circus.

The nightmare was over. Solomon Northup traveled back north to be reunited with his wife and kids, who were delighted and relieved to have him home.

For most people, one disappearance is enough. In Solomon Northup's case, he disappeared twice, and no one has ever solved the second mystery.

Solomon Northup toured the Northern states and even into Canada, talking about his experiences and the horrors of slavery. He wanted to help make slavery a thing of the past.

During the summer of 1857, in Streetsville, Ontario, an angry crowd prevented him from speaking. Maybe they were in favor of slavery and upset at Solomon Northup's stories of its horrors. History is quiet about this event.

Solomon Northup was never seen again.

What happened? No one knows.

Some say that Solomon Northup began a secret life helping slaves escape to freedom on the Underground Railroad. This secret system helped slaves escape from the South. It helped resettle runaway slaves in the free Northern states and Canada.

Did Solomon Northup join this group of abolitionists? If he decided to do this, he would have needed to fade from the bright public light he had focused on himself.

Some say he simply tired of traveling and speaking and went home to quietly live the rest of his life as a carpenter. But there are no records of this possibility and no stories about Solomon Northup in his old age.

Some say he was secretly killed in Canada by someone who wanted slavery to continue.

Did Solomon Northup disappear again to help people less fortunate than himself? Did he give up the fight to live his own life the way he wanted? We might never know.

As with most historical mysteries, people are still wondering what happened.

The final record of the long and strange life of Solomon Northup came in 1875, 10 years after President Abraham Lincoln ended slavery. A New York State Census lists his wife's marital status as "widowed," but it does not mention Solomon Northup, where he might have died, or how he might have died.

No grave of Solomon Northup has ever been found.

WHAT ELSE HAPPENED WHILE SOLOMON NORTHUP WAS A SLAVE?

- On March 4, 1841, William Henry Harrison is inaugurated president of the United States and gives a two-hour speech in frigid and wet weather. He catches pneumonia and dies 30 days later.

- Samuel F.B. Morse sends the first telegram from Washington, DC, to Baltimore, Maryland, on May 24, 1843.

- Abolitionist leader Frederick Douglass publishes his autobiography, *Narrative of the Life of Frederick Douglass: An American Slave*, in May 1845.

- Florida and Texas become states in 1845.

- Women's rights leader Amelia Bloomer causes a flurry of attention when she begins wearing loose fitting trousers under her skirt in 1845. The garments are called "bloomers."

- The first postage stamps with sticky backs are released in 1847.

- A worker at Sutter's sawmill in California makes an unusual discovery of gold in 1848. His discovery starts what will become known as the California Gold Rush.

- In 1850, the number of people living in the United States reaches more than 23 million.

- California becomes a state in 1850.

- Herman Melville publishes *Moby Dick* in 1851.

- Harriet Beecher Stowe publishes her anti-slavery novel, *Uncle Tom's Cabin,* in 1852. It sells more than 300,000 copies in three months.

abolitionist: a person supporting the end of slavery.

abundance: a very large quantity of something.

altitude: the height of something above the level of the sea; also called elevation.

ambitious: having a strong desire to succeed.

amendment: a correction, addition, or change to the U.S. Constitution.

auction: a public sale of property to the highest bidder.

aviator: a pilot.

bison: the correct name for an animal called the buffalo.

challenge: an invitation to compete or try to do something difficult.

chant: to repeat a sound over and over.

circulate: to pass from place to place or person to person.

circumnavigate: to go all the way around.

civilized: refers to people who are advanced in art, science, and politics.

colonist: a settler living in a new land.

colony: an area that is controlled by or belongs to another country.

community: a group of people who live in the same area.

complications: problems or difficulties.

contagious: easy to catch.

cower: to shrink away or cringe in fear.

crude: very basic.

current: the flow of water in a direction.

dervish: something that whirls or dances.

diphtheria: a contagious disease that can be fatal.

disappear: to vanish.

DNA: the substance in your cells that carries your genetic information, the "blueprint" of who you are. DNA tests can be used to identify people.

Glossary

empire: a group of countries controlled by one ruler.

engineer: someone who uses science, math, and creativity to solve problems.

epidemic: an outbreak of a disease that spreads quickly.

equator: an imaginary line around the earth, halfway between the North and South Poles.

era: a period of history marked by distinctive people or events.

evidence: something that proves, or could prove, the existence of something or the truth of an idea.

execute: to put to death.

exhilarate: to excite.

expedition: a trip taken by a group of people for a specific purpose such as exploration, scientific research, or war.

expertise: special skills or knowledge.

fatal: leading to death.

fate: the development of events beyond a person's control.

feat: a product of skill or endurance.

fraternal: a brotherhood or connection to fellow human beings.

front: the dividing point where two sides meet.

goods: things for sale or to use.

hardscrabble: involving struggle.

hesitation: pausing before doing or saying something.

horizon: the line in the distance where the land or sea seems to meet the sky.

humidity: the amount of moisture in the air.

immune: resistant to certain diseases.

indigenous: native to a place.

intervene: to alter the course of an event.

intrepid: fearless or adventurous.

intriguing: interesting.

Ku Klux Klan: a club organized in the South after the Civil War. It used violence against African Americans and other minority groups.

lurk: to remain hidden.

mainland: the land of a continent.

memoir: a historical account or biography written from personal knowledge.

mesmerized: fascinated by.

mistrust: to be suspicious of.

monarchy: a government ruled by a monarch—a king or queen.

monk: a religious man who lives a simple life to honor God.

navigator: a person in charge of choosing a travel route.

New World: the land now made up of North and South America. It was called the New World by people from Europe because it was new to them.

overseer: a person in charge of workmen as they work.

parasite: a living thing that feeds off another living thing.

peril: danger.

piranha: a fish with sharp teach that attacks animals.

provisions: supplies of food.

quarters: living space.

quiver: a case for arrows.

ransom: money demanded for the return of a captured person.

refinish: to redo something and make better.

remnant: a small, leftover piece of something.

resourceful: able to deal with new or difficult situations and to find solutions to problems.

restless: moving constantly.

reunite: to come together again.

Glossary

revenge: to hurt someone in exchange for an injury or wrong done to you or someone else.

revolution: an attempt to overthrow a government and replace it with a new system.

revolutionary: someone committed to fighting a ruler or political system.

rumor: a story or report of uncertain or doubtful truth.

sacrifice: to give something up for the sake of something else.

scarce: when there isn't enough of something.

settler: a person who is one of the first to live in an area.

sewer: a drain for wastewater.

shelter: a place to live that protects a person from the weather.

slave: a person owned by another person and forced to work without pay, against their will.

slog: to work hard during a period of time.

species: a group of living things that are closely related and produce young.

spiteful: growing hateful.

strive: to make a great effort.

territory: an area of land.

theory: an idea that tries to explain why something is the way it is.

theory of evolution: a scientific theory that explains how species change over time.

torturous: to involve pain and suffering.

trade: to exchange one thing for something else.

tsar: a Russian king.

uncertain: not known or open to question.

vaporize: to vanish.

voyage: a long trip by sea or in space.

wealth: money and valuable belongings.

Resources

Searching for Roanoke:
news.nationalgeographic.com/2015/08/150807-lost-colony-roanoke-hatteras-outer-banks-archaeology

Read an article from *National Geographic* about new evidence found by researchers searching for the lost colony of Roanoke!

Amelia Earhart:
ameliaearhart.com

Read more about Amelia Earhart and her journeys, plus take a look at how her life and legacy has lasted into today's world.

DNA Testing:
articles.latimes.com/2009/mar/11/science/sci-romanov11

You can read an article about the DNA testing that proved Anastasia Romanov was killed along with her family in 1918.

The Lost City of Z:
youtube.com/watch?v=pdTvh3GkO84

In 2017, film makers made an action movie called *The Lost City of Z* about Percy Fawcett's possible adventures in the Amazon. You can watch a trailer of the movie here.

12 Years a Slave:
docsouth.unc.edu/fpn/northup/northup.html

You can read the book written by Solomon Northup called *12 Years a Slave*. In it, he tells of his experiences being captured as a freeman and sold as a slave. The book can be found at this website.